THE PSYCHOLOGY OF RESEARCH WRITING

How to Overcome All Your Fears for Research Writing

MCWINNER YAWMAN, PHD.

The Psychology of Research Writing

How To Overcome All Your Fears For Research Writing

Published by
Yawman Book Publishing House
Davao Philippines

ISBN 978-1-329-65400-6

DEDICATION

This book is dedicated to my Children:
Ekyea, Kingtor, Ndaa, and Attra

FOREWORD

The fear of research writing is considered one of the greatest fears for most college and senior high school students today. Most students get very anxious and are gripped with fear when writing their thesis; this fear worsens during thesis defense or presentation.

This book will show you how I moved from the extreme fear of writing a thesis to an expert in research and publication and coached over 300 researchers to write and publish their research papers in SCOPUS, ISI-indexed, and other peer-reviewed journals.

The Psychology of Research Writing has been designed to help you overcome every fear of doing research. It will help you to believe in your ability to conduct outstanding research. This book is for college and senior high school students who are beginners in research writing. It is also an ideal companion for teachers who have a fear of research writing.

As a lifetime student and master of Neurolinguistic Programming, plus my experience in coaching hundreds of people to move from the fear of doing research to writing and publishing their papers, and having read and tested dozens of the best books and articles on the subject of the Psychology of Writing, I can surely bring you from where you are now to get you to write and publish your research paper.

For six years, I lived in Thailand - I had the opportunity to work with two leading universities. I conducted research and publication training for lecturers; did leadership training, camps, and coaching for different schools.

One common factor I noticed through those years of serving was that more than 90% of the people I dealt with were afraid of doing research. If they had other options than doing research, they would instead go for it.

There were times I met teachers who never wanted to pursue masters and doctoral degrees simply because they were afraid of doing research. Some never graduated with their master's degree simply because, according to them, writing a thesis was too difficult a thing to do.

Within these years, I developed the *Psychology of Research Writing Training*. With the training, I was able to help many lecturers and teachers write their papers and get them published in SCOPUS and ISI.

Of the truth, if you enter a university or college and survey students on what they think about writing a thesis, you will rarely find students or even teachers who love to do research. The question is – why is it like that?

CONTENTS

INTRODUCTION

I assumed the position of Research Director as a young man full of zeal, willing to do everything to help create the research culture in the college. It was my first day of class. I was wondering how my class was going to be like!

Then the lesson began; I asked my class, "What is research?" The class was quiet for some time, and then to my surprise, one of the boys lifted his hand, so I permitted him to say what he thinks about research.

The student gave a fantastic answer; the answer was not correct, though. However, it was an eye-opener for me. The student boldly answered my question, "Research is difficult." That was his definition of research.

This made me realize that I had something more serious to deal with in the students than teaching lessons on research. The students' perception and beliefs about research needed to be dealt with first before any lesson on research are introduced.

In the students' minds, the definition of research was like this:

RESEARCH = DIFFICULT

Now I had to find a way to help my students re-orient their minds before teaching any lesson on research.

I asked the class, "How many of you like adventure?"

Almost every hand in the class went up. Then, I asked a second question, "How many of you like to discover new things?" Again, almost every hand went up. I asked them," Is adventure fun?" They said, "Yes." "How about discovering new things? Is it fun?" They said, "Yes."

After this, I continued. "...this is how research is - It is both an **adventure** and the **discovery** of new things."

Then I asked more questions, "Do people cry on adventures?" The class answered, "Yes." "Despite all the crying, is it still fun?" They answered yes. "Now you have well understood the concepts," I said.

What would it be if you were asked to give the word or phrase to describe discovery and adventure?

*It is challenging but **fun, fun, and fun.***

Out of this, we got a new representation for research in the minds of the students:

RESEARCH = ADVENTURE + DISCOVERY + FUN

If the mind gets it right, everything will go right. On the other hand, if it gets it wrong, everything can go wrong.

The Psychology of Research Writing you are about to read has been proven to create positive, long-lasting results. All you have to do to master the psychology of research writing is to keep reading. Every chapter will give you new insights to help you master the skill quickly.

SECTION I

The 3 Keys You Must Master as a Researcher

"In almost every career or field <u>80 percent of all success is due to psychology—mindset, beliefs, and emotions and only 20 percent is due to strategy or mechanics</u>—the specific steps needed to accomplish a result" - Anthony Robins

With the right vision, passion, and mindset, your chances of successfully finishing your research project are exponentially greater, no matter the difficulties you will face.

CHAPTER 1

Believe You Can Write a Great Research

As a student, self-belief can be a powerful tool for you if you understand its place in personal achievement. Belief is the fuel that propels you towards success in research writing.

As a researcher, you can accomplish extraordinary things as long as you have the correct belief.

The Encarta dictionary explains "belief" as the "acceptance by the mind that something is true or real, often underpinned by an emotional or spiritual sense of certainty." [1]

This definition points out the dimensions of beliefs. It embraces all aspects of who you are: mental, emotional, physical, and spiritual.

As a student, you form beliefs about a particular subject or course right from childhood because of certain experiences in school. These beliefs can often stay with you for a lifetime and prevent you from advancing in certain areas of your life.

Belief is multi-dimensional, and that is why it is crucial to understand it very well.

Your beliefs about school, teachers, courses, and the like are the lens through which you view your ability to excel.

Your beliefs can:

1. Influence your perceptions about research

2. Direct or limit the actions you take in research writing

3. Shape your attitude in research writing

4. Affect your relationships with your team members

5. Establish a specific course you will follow as a student

6. Harness or hijack your passion for research

Every student lives within and operates out of a complex set of beliefs that define them and their ability to excel in conducting research.

Your beliefs about research are your reality-making blueprint—they will determine whether you will take action or not. Your beliefs about research will produce an equivalent level of excellence for you as a student.

Anything you believe to be true becomes your experience most of the time. Most students hardly sit down to question their beliefs and why they dislike some particular subjects in school. As long as you do not challenge your beliefs as a student, they will shape your perceptions and direct your actions at a subliminal or subconscious level.

Your fate in particular courses is more or less sealed—or, to be more accurate, your reality-making process is governed by your beliefs.

"Belief always precedes action." – James Allen.[2] Since your beliefs determine how you take action, positive beliefs about your ability to do research are more likely to foster actions and attitudes that attract positive outcomes.

Likewise, negative beliefs about research are likely to foster attitudes and actions or inactions which contrary to conducting great research.

Negative beliefs are like viruses. If you embrace them, they will destroy your self-confidence in your ability to do research.

This is the good news: your experience in past researches does not matter; you can re-orient your mind now and take a new course toward writing a great research project.

In the next paragraph, I explain what limiting beliefs are. You might be familiar with limiting beliefs, or maybe not.

CHAPTER 2

Overcoming Your Limiting Beliefs in Research Writing

Limiting beliefs are wrong beliefs that people have about something. Usually, these beliefs prevent them from taking action to help them succeed in a particular area. It is a wrong mindset about something because of some experiences in the past.

Most new researchers have many limiting beliefs about research and publication. These limiting beliefs prevent them from taking the proper steps and actions to do research. Most students never engage in research because of the wrong mindsets.

Some common limit beliefs about research and publication:

1. Research is difficult
2. Research is hard
3. I don't know how to do research

4. I don't know where to begin
5. I am not an expert in research
6. Research is hell
7. Research is stressful
8. I don't need research
9. I don't know where to get data
10. I can't analyze data
11. I don't have funding for research
12. I don't know whom to talk to about my research
13. I am not ready for research yet
14. I don't have time. I am too busy
15. I don't know what topic to choose

Students have countless limiting beliefs. These beliefs become the foundation for their research.

You will never get started with a wrong foundation or mindset, not to talk about writing a great research project.

How to Overcome Your Limiting Beliefs about Research and Publication

As I mentioned earlier, limiting beliefs are formed from bad experiences or lies accepted as truth in the past. People form limiting believes primarily

to stay safe or to help them stay in their comfort zone. Most limiting beliefs are lies, and that once you let them go, you will find it more fulfilling to live without them. A recent study by Harvard University showed that less than 2% of people ever reach their dreams.

This is because most people are unwilling to leave their comfort zones and pay the price to achieve their dreams; this applies to students. You will need new beliefs about research writing to be able to excel in it.

Now let us closely examine the limiting beliefs mentioned earlier.

1. Research is difficult

Many students think research is difficult, so they ultimately give up on conducting research projects. Other students do not entirely give up; however, they hardly write great projects because of their negative attitudes.

Now let us face the fact. Is research challenging? The answer is **YES** and **NO**. It can be challenging for you as a student if you do not know what to do. This is also true for any other project or business. However, if you know what to do, whom to talk to, whom to collaborate with, where to get your data from, and all that, conducting research can be extremely fun.

I say this because conducting research is both an adventure and a discovery with fun. However, you need to understand that both adventure and discovery are challenging in some way too. This difficulty does not eliminate fun.

People who go for adventure always focus on fun, and remember that where focus goes, energy flows to trigger that emotion.

If your focus is on the difficulty, you will find it extremely tough. However, if your focus is on discovery and fun, you will find it challenging yet super fun.

You have to focus on your outcome or the fun you will gain from the project rather than the occasional difficulties you will go through.

2. I don't know how to do research

This is one of the common sayings of students. The question is, "Do you need to know everything

about research before you begin?" Maybe not. Every scientific inquiry involves steps. And as a student, you need to learn to master one step at a time.

In my class, I use this metaphor to calm down my students. I ask them, "How many of you can eat a cow in a day?" Every time I ask this question, I get no answer. On the other hand, if I ask, "How many of you can eat a cow in a year? Almost every hand goes up."

I continue to explain that doing research can be very overwhelming if you try to do everything at once. It is essential to break the tasks into small actionable steps. With this, you work on it a little at a time. Just know how to do one task at a time, and you will write a great research project.

Secondly, doing research is teamwork. It would be best to focus on what you can do best and delegate or consult on tasks you are not good at. You might find it useful to hire a statistician to analyze your data than spending a whole week learning how to use SPSS or other software.

3. I do not know where to begin

I have heard dozens of students and teachers make this comment. In reply to that, I make this joke, "Well, if you do not know where to begin

with your research, just pick a stone and throw it. Just begin at where the stone lands". Lots of laughs!

I am certain you have some personal experience or have seen some problems in your field that need to be solved. Any of those could be your starting point; it should not be a big project.

The most important thing is that your study is relevant and contributes to knowledge. Just look around you – in school, classroom, home, community, workplace, etc.; are there any problems that need to be investigated?

You could also read studies that have been conducted in your field. And you will notice the problems or areas that have not been studied yet.

4. I am not an expert in research

You don't have to be an expert to do research. With the little knowledge you have, you can get started. There is no perfect research, so don't worry about perfection. Your goal is to write great research – research that solves a problem or contributes to the body of knowledge.

If your goal is to be an expert before you begin your research project, you might never get started; you become an expert by doing, not by talking.

Don't worry about making mistakes and all that. They are part of the research process.

5. Research is hell

Once in a while, you will hear students make comments like that. The truth is that anything can be hell if you see it like hell.

You can choose to call the problems you go through challenges or just questions to be solved.

Every problem is simply a question that has not been answered yet. You can switch your mind from thinking you are having problems with your research to thinking you have some questions that need to be answered. This is important because every time you think about problems, your mind begins to worry; on the other hand, every time you think about questions, your mind goes searching for answers.

Equate the problems you encounter in writing research to challenges or questions. In this way, you will not feel like hell. Rather, you will talk to people who can help you find the answers you need for your project.

6. Research is stressful

Yes, it can be! As much as you want to do everything by yourself, you will surely stress

yourself.

As mentioned earlier, doing research involves collaboration. Don't be a "jack of all trade," as this will lead to stress. Focus on the key things you can do best and delegate the rest. Be sure to consult your advisers as well.

Talk to them about anything you don't understand, and they will help you out.

There is no need to sit down and stress yourself trying to figure out something.

For ethical reasons, you should understand that the "what," except data analysis. An expert can do the data analysis.

7. I don't need research

Your ability to do research is a skill that will be useful in your entire life. Most successful businesses are born out of research.

Whether you want to start your own business or apply for a job, your ability to do research will highly boost your success rate. The skill of doing research is a trait that almost every company looks for in hiring employees. Understanding this helps you develop a good attitude to mastering how to write a great research.

8. I don't know where to get data

Getting data for research can be difficult if you want it to be. That is why there are sampling methods and data gathering tools. These tools are supposed to help you get the data you need for your research. As a beginner, you do not need to think about very big data that is difficult to manage or access.

Begin with manageable data using sampling tools that are easy to understand. Choose a research environment that allows easy access to data so you will not have a problem getting your data. As you gain experience, you can consider bigger and more complex data.

9. I can't analyze data

Analyzing your data should not be a problem at all. In school, we never study the same course.

Some specialize in statistics, others in biology and business, and so on. If you are a biology student, just give your data to the statistician to analyze it for you. After that, you can proceed to write the discussion.

You might not know how to use software to analyze statistical data; however, that doesn't mean you cannot do research. In very

sophisticated systems, specialization is the key to productivity. People are trained to be the best in one area.

You could always hire someone to help you with your data analysis. I have personally hired some for my statistical analysis, and I will continue to use their services. I focus on my strengths and hire someone to take care of the other areas.

10. I don't have funding for research

Research can be costly; however, it doesn't mean you need much funding before you think about doing research. As a beginner, you don't need to think about that.

It would be best to always think of simple research you will not have to spend so much money conducting. As you gain experience and learn how to apply for research grants, you could think about doing research that involves big data.

It is very important to take the resources you have into consideration when planning your research. There is no need to get into a project in which your present resources cannot support it.

The good news is that most universities and colleges have systems in place to support institutional research. Thus, if you can write a good research proposal, your institution will likely fund your project.

A type of research that might involve little or no cost at all is using secondary data sources. Some examples are doing literature review or paper critiquing, writing short communication, and literature analysis. With these kinds of research, you might not spend much. If your school cannot fund your project and you can't personally support it, then use secondary data sources.

11. I don't know whom to talk to about my research

Whom to talk to should not be a problem at all. Probably at your school, you have a research department. Just go to the department and speak to the research director. Tell him or her about the research you want to do. He will assign you to a professor who will mentor you in your project to completion.

12. I am not ready for research yet

I met a female teacher who said, "I am not ready for research yet." So I asked her, "What need to happen for you to be ready for research?"

She gave reasons upon reasons. I had to be honest with her, so I told her that research writing is now an integral part of every college and university. The government is pushing all institutions to get involved in research because it is the heart of the innovation and growth of every country.

Research has now become a criterion for accreditation in higher education institutions.

Teachers who will not learn how to do research and publish papers will soon be replaced.

All companies and organizations need research for growth and expansion, so you will always have the upper hand and be promoted faster if you harness your research skill.

13. I don't have time, I am too busy

There is always time for everything. Just say yes to one thing and no to other things. Learn also how to manage your time well. It means you will have to set priorities, schedule time for your research project, commit to action, and never postpone.

Reasons Why You Must Believe in Your Ability to Do Research

It is your perspective that defines how you think about yourself. Your frequent thoughts create your life as a student. Your thought pattern for the past years has created your present achievement. If you want to achieve greater success, you need to believe in your ability to succeed. Who you will be in the future is all up to you.

1. Your competence as a student and whom you will become after graduation depends on you and no one else. The truth is, you are in full control of your career. So understand that no one can achieve your goals for you. You are the only one who can achieve your dreams. No one else will do them for you. You MUST believe you can do research knowing how relevant research skill is to the success of your career and life.

2. After you believe, your mind will be tuned to work to succeed in doing research. With a proper mindset, you will see challenges as opportunities to learn, attract different ways of moving towards your success and notice more options for moving forward.

3. Believing in your ability to do research is the only force to get you started and keep your momentum. Let every bit of belief in you drive you to take action toward writing your research.

4. Your self-belief or believing in your ability to accomplish great things is your greatest asset as a student. Never treat yourself as a weakling or a student with weak mental capacity, as this can subconsciously ruin your entire life.

5. Choosing to believe you can write great research will drive you and inspire you. Athletes train for years because they believe they can win the race. Dare to believe!

Successful researchers/writers believe in themselves and their ability to complete their projects. And most of all, they understand the power of beliefs to determine the actions they need to take. "Whether you think you can, or you think you can't – you're right"- Henry Ford.

Believe you have what it takes to conduct great research, be proud of your project, and like what you are doing.

Examining yourself

1. Do you believe you can write a great research project within your set time? _____

_____

_____

_____

_____

_____

2. On a scale of 1 to 10, how confident are you to write a great project? _____

_____

_____

_____

_____

_____

3. What needs to happen for you to have a confidence level of 10 in writing a great research project?

_____

_____

_____

_____

_____

4. Based on your answers in question 3 above, what MUST you do to raise your confidence level to 10?

_____

_____

_____

_____

_____

5. What possible problems/hindrances do you need to overcome to write an outstanding project?

_____

_____

_____

_____

_____

Now take the necessary action steps to overcome all possible setbacks you might encounter

CHAPTER 3

Have a Good Attitude Toward Your Research Project

Attitude is simply a predisposition or a tendency to respond positively or negatively towards a certain idea, object, person, or situation. Your attitude influences your choice of action and how you respond to challenges, incentives, and rewards.

It is also a mindset or a tendency to act in a particular way due to both an individual's experience and temperament. Your attitudes will help you define how you see situations and behave toward the situation or object.

Four major components of attitude are

(1) Affective: emotions or feelings.
(2) Cognitive: belief or opinions held consciously.
(3) Conative: inclination for action.
(4) Evaluative: positive or negative response to stimuli.[1]

Your attitudes will influence your decisions, guide your behavior, and impact the level to which you embrace new things or challenging tasks.

The attitudes you bring to work will determine whether you will succeed or not. You will need to have specific attitudes that the most successful researchers share in common, like courage, persistence, adaptability, curiosity, willingness to take action and more risk, collaboration, focus, self-fulfillment, and the desire to succeed.

Will you muster the courage to defend your project and your results?

_____

_____

_____

How will you do that?

_____

_____

_____

Robert Biswas-Diener, the author of The Courage Quotient, mentioned that courage is a skill, and like all skills, it can be learned, strengthened, and mastered with repeated practice.

Building courage is a little bit like building muscle; the more you use it, the stronger it gets.

Otherwise, the more it shrivels. As a researcher, you can build courage continuously by talking about your project with your peers and advisers. In this way, all potential questions will be asked, and you will have the opportunity to answer them before your defense.[2]

Persistence is one of the key attitudes that will determine whether you will complete your project or not. Many students do not finish their projects because they don't persist enough and usually give up when frustrations arise.

No great achievement is possible without persistent work. – Bertrand Russell

A distinguishing trait of great researchers in academia is persistence. Many researchers set goals and make plans for their projects, yet only a few finishes them because only a few sticks to work on their goals and plans until they are completed.

Many students quit in the middle of their projects. They let their fears and doubts prevent them from moving persistently toward their project goals. Other students lack the motivation it takes to keep moving.

The following will help you to build persistence:

1. Know the importance of your project. What will you get after completion? What is your motivation?

You should know WHY the project MUST be done. Keep your eyes on the benefits of your project.

2. Have a Positive Mindset

Writing great research is challenging; that is why only a few people do research. There will be countless times you will face difficulties and might give up if you are not persistent.

To develop the persistence to succeed, always maintain a positive mental attitude, no matter your situation. Keep your thoughts focused on taking action towards your goals.

3. Associate with Researchers

Be sure to surround yourself with people who are doing research. You could create a mastermind group wherein you can meet to share ideas on your project's progress regularly.[3]

Evaluating yourself

How well can you persist until you finish your project? Rate yourself from 1 to 10.

_____

If you feel like quitting, what will you do to keep going?

_____
_____
_____
_____
_____
_____

Your ability to adapt to everyday changes in your research environment is very important. How flexible you are counts a lot. There will be times you will need to make changes to your work. Other times, your advisers could even ask you to start all over again. In situations like this, will you continue? For example, in gathering data, you might have to travel to other cultures or communities. Mingling in new cultures might not always be fun. These are the fact you will need to know to get your mind ready. It would be best if you were adaptable.

26

Evaluating yourself

Are you adaptable?

_____

_____

_____

How adaptable are you? Give yourself a score. (1-10)

_____

_____

What do you need to do to improve your adaptability?

_____

_____

_____

_____

_____

_____

Researchers are curious most of the time; it has to do with your willingness to go the extra mile until you get what you want. It's also about not stopping to ask more questions – what's in there? You need to be curious to write a great project.

How curious are you? Give yourself a score (1-10)

_____

_____

What do you need to increase your curiosity?

_____

_____

_____

_____

_____

_____

_____

"Taking action" is what separates winners from losers, great researchers from mere researchers, and the rich from the poor. Achievers are action and risk-takers. As a researcher, you should be willing to take more action and risks to achieve great results.

Are you an action taker or a procrastinator?

_____

_____

_____

_____

_____

Are you willing to take risks to achieve great results?

_____

_____

_____

_____

_____

What needs to happen for you to take more action and risk? _____

_____

_____

_____

_____

_____

Collaboration is very vital in every project. Your ability to work in teams will highly determine your success. Many research projects involve partnership and cooperation between two or more people. You will have to harness this skill to be successful. You need to understand that people have different temperaments, backgrounds, training, culture, and the like. Working with people like this might not be convenient at all. However, if you are a people-oriented person, you will learn to collaborate irrespective of your differences. Collaboration is also a skill that you will need to master to help you achieve great results.

How well can you collaborate with others? Give yourself a score (1-10).

_____

_____

How well are you able to work with people from different backgrounds?

_____

_____

_____

_____

What will you do to improve your ability to collaborate? _____

_____

_____

_____

_____

_____

_____

_____

_____

_____

CHAPTER 4

Master How to Stay Focused on Your Research Project

As a student or researcher, for sure, you have many tasks to work on. Staying focused can be difficult, knowing you have other assignments and projects that need your attention. That is why you need to master how to remain focused to increase your productivity.[1]

To stay focused, understand that when you say YES to one task, you have to say NO to all other tasks at that particular moment. It means that elimination is a prerequisite for focus. Tim Ferriss puts it this way, "What you don't do determines what you can do." [2]

Lack of focus is one of the greatest enemies of productivity in writing research. Constant distractions will lower your performance and make you waste your time and energy. Being productive is not a question of how much time in a day you spend working, but much you get done or accomplish.[3]

If there is one key trait of a successful researcher, it is the ability to focus all attention over some time. Research has shown that the mind can concentrate well on only one thing at a time. Therefore, stay on one thing; finish it before you pick up another task. Multiple projects, most of the time, never get completed in one sitting.

When the astrophysicist Jaymice Matthews was interviewed, he said, "Focus is the single keyword for success." " According to Tom Monagham, the founder of Domain Pizza, the secret of his success is a fanatical focus on doing one thing well. Successful researchers are not great at everything; they are great at only one thing; this is focusing (specializing) on just one single task at a time.

Bill Gates once said, "If you want to be a great software company, you have to be only a software company. You can't dabble another thing." Be an expert at something, just one thing.

Are you a person who stay focused until the task at hand is finished? _____

_____

_____

_____

_____

_____

How much will you rate yourself on your ability to focus? (1-10)   _____

_____

_____

_____

What needs to happen to help you get more focused?   _____

_____

_____

_____

_____

_____

These tips can help you focus:

1. Set daily research goals. For every day, set specific goals for your project and commit to accomplishing those tasks.

2. Chunk down big tasks into easily manageable small tasks. It will not make you feel overwhelmed when working on them.

3. Schedule all tasks. Tasks that are not scheduled might never get done. Set a particular

time in the day for the task to be accomplished and ensure you are not distracted by anything.

4. Remove all distractions. Choose a place where you will not be disturbed or distracted. If you are working on a computer, close all unnecessary applications like social media sites and work full screen to eliminate distractions.

SECTION II:

The Iceberg Theory Of Achievement

The Iceberg Theory of Achievement (ITA)

The ITA teaches that every great educator, academician, professor, or researcher invested a lot of effort and time and worked hard to succeed. Knowing this as a student will make you more persistent and do whatever it takes to reach your academic goals and finish your research successfully.

The ITA requires that for you as a researcher to write a great research project and get it published, you must understand the seven concepts/pillars that work together to guarantee achievement. Nothing great comes without a cost.

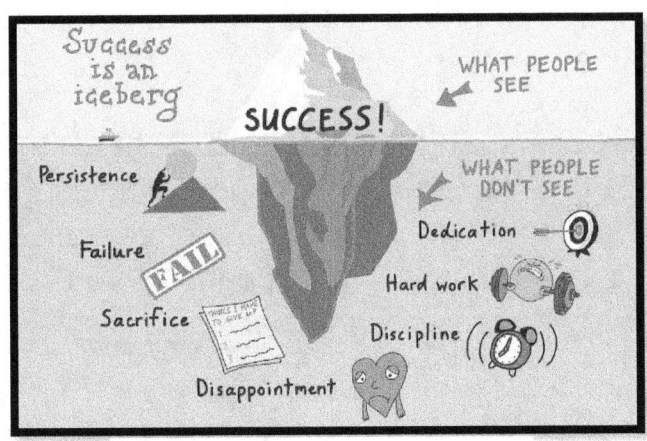

Source: https://businessideaslab.com

CHAPTER 5

Stay Committed to Your Research Project till You are Done

Commitment is the state or quality of being dedicated to a cause or an activity. Commitment like self-discipline is one of the bridges between goals and achievement. If you don't get committed, there is no way you will finish your research. After you start your research, many things will try to steal your time or get your attention. It will take great commitment to be able to stay on track.

Many teachers and faculty find it hard to do research or write academic papers because of a lack of commitment. You may have research goals, but nothing will happen if you don't commit to your research goals.

Some facts to help you get committed to your research:

1. Program your mind to think right. Your ability to write great research begins with

your mindset. Negative beliefs about your ability to do research will paralyze your self-confidence and tendency to take action.

To give your best and make great progress, you must make a personal decision that you will not let anything hold you back. Envision what you will have after you have finished your project and decide that you will let nothing impede the success of your project; this is the first step in getting committed to your project.

2. Set very clear and realistic research goals

It's usually hard to commit to something that you are not sure about. That is why setting clear research goals is very important. What exactly do you want to achieve from your research?

Apart from the results of your research project, you should have a clear picture of the benefits you will attain for undertaking that project. For example, will it bring a promotion or an increased salary, among others? Setting a realistic goal also means you are going to work within a time frame. Ensure that the goals you have set for your project can be achieved within the time frame to avoid stress and frustration. Do well to set monthly, weekly and daily goals for your project.

3. Always focus on the important tasks

As a researcher, do first things first. Prioritize the most important tasks in your project and delegate the less important ones. In doing research, you don't have to go ahead of yourself. Follow the proper order of research writing; move to the next stage only after completing one task. You don't have to nibble at many tasks and leave them uncompleted.

You may want to ask yourself a question like, "If I could work on just one task for today, what would be it?" With this question, your mind will automatically look for the most important task on your list. You could also make use of Pareto's 80/20 principle.

4. Be accountable to yourself and your mentors

For most people, willpower is not strong enough to get them to follow through on their commitments. Your initial motivation is good enough to get you started. However, to follow through, you are going to need something more. To stay committed, you need a way to hold yourself accountable.

Be sure to have a personal adviser for your project. You should also tell your peers to hold you accountable for your daily or weekly tasks. Surrounding yourself with like-minded people who are into research can be extremely helpful. It can provide you with the confidence and motivation you need to take your project to a whole new level.[1]

How well are you able to commit to tasks you start till they are completed?

_____

_____

_____

Give yourself a score (1-10)

_____

_____

What will you do to help you get committed to your research project until it's completed?

_____

_____

_____

_____

CHAPTER 6

Understand Doing Research is Hard Work

There is no great research without hard work. Hard work is always the baseline of great breakthroughs in research. Getting things organized, setting goals, making plans to achieve them, and staying on track all involve hard work.

Rarely do researchers fail to achieve their goals with the hard work approach. You might be very inexperienced now, but with hard work, you can produce great results.

Some people think there are shortcuts to achieving great things. I do not believe there is any shortcut to greatness. If ever there is, it might be only one: using the wisdom and counsel of mentors.

Understand that the "process" is more important than "results." If you miss the process, the results are meaningless because you cannot justify them.

There are no shortcuts to lasting success. Some students will do what is easiest and avoid hard work— this is not a good idea.

You do not have to produce a project you are not proud of. Great research can only be achieved through hard work. This means if you do not have the skill, you should learn it or seek an expert's advice.

Jim Rohn, America's foremost business philosopher, puts it this way, "Don't wish it were easier; wish you were better".

Some notable sayings about hard work

Stephen King – "Talent is cheaper than table salt. What separates the talented individual from the successful one is a lot of hard work."

Henry Ford – "The harder you work, the luckier you get, and you become more successful."

In doing research, there is no substitute for hard work. You might have heard about people winning the best thesis and great awards – know that greatness is not just awarded to anyone; it requires much hard work. The best researchers in any field are those who devote time and work hard on their projects.

Hard work can be challenging or even uncomfortable. As a researcher, you must not hate challenging tasks or projects because they come with great opportunities most of the time.

I am certain you know of the famous Thomas Edison who failed approximately 10,000 times while working on the light bulb, yet he never dreamed of giving up—this is the hard work I am talking of. Edison achieved great results because he was committed to hard work. According to Edison, the three great essentials to achieve anything worthwhile are hard work, stick-to-itiveness, and common sense.

As a researcher or student, you do not need to oppose hard work; instead, run with it and be proud of yourself. Your life will reach a whole new level when you stop avoiding hard work and simply embrace it.

It is important to understand that every research project involves hard work. You must understand this before you even start to write your proposal. Without hard work, you won't be able to finish your project successfully.[1]

Assessing yourself

Are you the type of person who embraces hard work?

_____

_____

_____

_____

How much will you rate yourself when it comes to embracing hard work? (1-10)

_____

_____

_____

_____

What will you do differently to help you change the attitude of abhorring hard work?

_____

_____

_____

_____

_____

_____

_____

_____

CHAPTER 7

You Must Master Yourself (Self-Discipline)

"If you wouldn't follow yourself, why should anyone else?" - John C. Maxwell

Self-discipline is gaining control of oneself and conduct, usually for personal improvement.

It is one of the most important and useful attributes every great researcher or outstanding student possesses. This attribute is essential, and without it, you cannot complete any great research project.

Self-discipline gives you the power to stick to your decisions and follow them through without changing your mind and is, therefore, one of the important requirements for achieving great results. On the other hand, a lack of self-discipline in you as a researcher, will lead to failure in finishing your research project.

Mastering yourself to finish your project is true power. Remember that the first person you must lead in conducting your research is you. If you can succeed in doing this, you can master any other task in your project.

Accomplishing your daily tasks and following through with the little things you set yourself to do will move you ahead in completing your project.

As you become disciplined, you act by reasoning, not by feeling. You work on your project despite all the challenges you may encounter. It often involves sacrificing the pleasure and thrill of the moment for what matters most to you – your project.

Self-discipline, like a muscle, can be developed. If you were raised in a disciplined environment, you might find it easier to be self-disciplined; nonetheless, as I mentioned earlier, this skill is learnable.

Check out these helpful suggestions below

1. Do not wait to feel like it; do it because it has to be done.

2. Finish what you start, one task at a time.

3. Dump the excuses. Be honest with yourself, and just do it.

4. No negotiation. Do what is assigned for every moment. Do not do what you have not planned or scheduled.

5. Set a deadline for every task, and live by them. Do everything possible to work within the schedule.

6. Set priorities; put first things first. Do not waste time on things that do not contribute to your goal in any way.

7. Arrest all the "time vampires." Remember that breakfast comes before dinner; do not mess things up.

Self-discipline has to do with your ability to perform the tasks that need to be completed, whether you feel at it or not. Until your project is completed, you must exercise as much self-control as possible. It also means you will remove all forms of distractions and things that could compete for your time.

How disciplined are you as a person? Give yourself a score (1-10).

_____

_____

_____

What can you do to master the skill of self-discipline?

_____

_____

_____

_____

_____

_____

_____

_____

_____

_____

CHAPTER 8

Anticipate Disappointment in One Area or the Other

Disappointment is simply the feeling of sadness or displeasure when people don't fulfill your hopes or expectations. Every researcher is likely to face some kind of disappointment in the process of writing a research project.

Since your research project involves many people, there is always the likelihood that someone in your team, your advisers, or respondents might fail to perform their tasks or responsibilities. It would be best always to have backup plans on what to do if there is a disappointment.

Just be careful not to let disappointment create resentment and hurt in your relationship with your advisers, team, or respondents. You might not be able to avoid disappointment completely; you need to learn how to deal with it.[1]

A common way to deal with disappointment is to practice gratitude. Always keep your mind on your positive progress and be thankful for it. Take note of all the little acts of kindness, the little assistance, and favors you receive from people doing your project, and be grateful for them.

Another way to deal with disappointment is to manage your expectations. Naturally, it is not practical to expect every event to turn out according to your plan. If you live by this philosophy, you are setting yourself up for disappointments most of the time. It does not mean you should not be positive. You should be positive, of course, and do your very best. If things do not go according to plan, you should still feel great knowing you did your very best.

Disappointments are natural consequences of taking risks. Sometimes you will win, sometimes you will be disappointed. That's how things are. Just get used to this fact as you begin your research project.[2]

Assessing yourself

On a scale of 1-10, how well are you able to handle disappointment?

_____

_____

_____

What will you do to improve your ability to
handle disappointment as a researcher?

_____

_____

_____

_____

_____

_____

_____

CHAPTER 9

Give Up to Go Up (Sacrifice)

To sacrifice for your thesis means you will give up time, energy, and resources to complete your project. Most research involves long hours of work, much energy, and resources. You will have to estimate how much sacrifice you will need to make before you begin your project.

Many sacrifices come into mind when one thinks about research. I will talk about just two main sacrifices you will make to complete your research project.

1. Sacrifice Personal Interests

To avail of much time for your research project, you will have to take a break from some of the "time vampires" in your day. Typical of them are Facebook, video games, television series, movies, window shopping, football, and other trivial activities that your life does not depend on them. This might be hard to say, but it is true;

every successful researcher knows and embraces the fact that certain personal interests need to be abandoned to accomplish great success as a researcher. It does not mean you leave them for good; it simply means you do not spend long hours on them after committing to complete a project.

There is not anything like "nothing for something." Every great accomplishment comes with some sacrifice; this is what I mean by "giving up to go up".[1]

2. Sacrifice Time

I have repeatedly heard students and teachers at my training and seminars say that "they cannot conduct research because they don't have time. They are too busy. Almost every time, I ask, "how many hours in a day do you have?" After their answer, I ask again, "how many hours does Donald Trump have? Who needs to complain about time, you or Donald Trump?

One thing you must understand is this – there is time for everything you want to accomplish. Just learn this: if you say yes to one thing, learn to say no to every other thing until your commitment is completed. It's all about how you use your time. There are too many things to do in a day, and therefore it's not about having enough time. It's about making good use of your time. We all have the same 24 hours, and we all have the opportunity to use our time wisely. How come someone makes $1,000 an hour while others make $10 in an hour? It's all about using your time well. When you sacrifice your time, you're setting priority for what's most important to you.

You will need to set daily research goals (write to-do lists) every single day and stick to them. Be sure to schedule every item on your list and set deadlines for them. Honor your word and do not procrastinate. You don't have to get involved in things that are not part of your daily goals.[2]

Are you the type of person who makes great sacrifices to get what he/she wants?

_____

_____

_____

On a scale of 1-10, how will you rate your willingness to sacrifice for your research project?

_____

_____

_____

_____

What needs to happen for you to sacrifice to complete your project?

_____

_____

_____

_____

_____

CHAPTER 10

Anticipate Failure

You need to anticipate some form of failure as you carry out your project. Make your mind up that you will not give up no matter the number of failures you encounter. Turn those failures into feedback, and find out what went wrong so that those failures don't happen again. Let the failures be your stepping stones, and learn from them.

Let me tell you some stories of people who failed many times in their pursuit of results. Before these people succeeded, they failed remarkably, not once or twice, but many times. Be inspired, and embrace failure as merely a chance to learn new ways for producing great results.

Meet Sir James Dyson, the inventor and designer

Sir Dyson tells how he bought the most powerful vacuum cleaner on the market in the late 1970s – the Hoover Junior. According to him, he got irritated when it started losing suction and tore the bag open. Its pores were clogged with dust –

a fundamental flaw but valuable to the industry because it meant consumers continually had to buy new bags.

He tells of how he was at a local sawmill one day and noticed how large industrial cyclones removed the sawdust from the air. He thought if that could work on a smaller scale. To create a solution, he made a cardboard prototype and strapped it onto his machine. It didn't look great, though, but it picked up more dust.

He continued through 5,000 failures for 15 years and finally had a bagless vacuum cleaner. By that point, though, he was heavily in debt and didn't know where to turn to bring his machine to the market.

At this point, he received a call from a Japanese company, Apex. He met them and signed a deal. In 1986, the production of the G-force began and won a prize. The invention was very successful in Japan. In less than two years, he launched the DC01, the first Dyson vacuum cleaner. It was soon a bestseller.

Sir James Dyson went through failures for 15 years before creating his eponymous best-selling bagless vacuum cleaner that led to a net worth of $4.5billion.[1,2]

What lessons have you learned from Sir James Dyson?

As a researcher, what will you do when you encounter failure?

Meet Thomas Edison

I am sure you have heard about the great Scientist, Thomas Edison. He is considered a master of "trial and error." When he was asked about the many thousands of failures he had when trying to create the light-bulb, he famously said, "I have not failed. I've just found 10,000 ways that won't work".

It is said that Thomas Edison was not the inventor of the first light bulb; however, he came up with the technology that helped bring it to the masses. Edison was motivated to perfect a commercially practical, efficient incandescent light bulb modeling Humphry Davy's invention, the first electric arc lamp in the early 1800s.

For over decades, following Davy's creation, scientists such as Warren de la Rue, Joseph Wilson Swan, Henry Woodward, and Mathew Evans had worked to perfect electric light bulbs or tubes using a vacuum but were unsuccessful in their attempts.

After Edison bought Woodward and Evans' patent and made improvements in his design, he was granted a patent for his improved light bulb in 1879. He started to manufacture and market it for widespread use. In January 1880, he had the vision to build a company that would supply electricity to power and light many cities.

That same year, Edison birthed the Edison Illuminating Company — the first investor-owned electric utility. It later became the General Electric Corporation. In 1881, he left Menlo Park to establish facilities in several cities where electrical systems were installed. In 1882, the Pearl Street generating station provided 110 volts of electrical power to 59 customers in lower Manhattan.

In 1878, Edison focused on inventing a safe, inexpensive electric light to replace the gaslight – a challenge scientists grappled with for the last 50 years. With the help of prominent financial backers like J.P. Morgan and the Vanderbilt family, Edison set up the Edison Electric Light Company and began research and development. He made a breakthrough in October 1879 with a bulb that used a platinum filament. In the summer of 1880, it hit on carbonized bamboo as a viable alternative for the filament, which proved to be the key to a long-lasting and affordable light bulb. In 1881, he set up an electric light company in Newark, and the following year moved his family (which by now included three children) to New York.[3,4]

What have you learned from the story of Thomas Edison?

Like Thomas Edison, how can you take one idea and develop it to a whole new level through innovation?

Meet Stephen King

King was working as a teacher in rural Maine when he wrote his first novel, "Carrie." King had some success selling short stories previously, but nothing to create a career from it.

King was rejected 30 times. After writing the book, he sent it out to 30 publishers; all publishers rejected his work.

In 1974 King was a frustrated writer; he crumpled up his three-page work and dumped it. Before his 31st attempt, he threw the manuscript out. His wife rescued it from the round file and asked him to try one more time. The rest is history. King gave up writing because life was hard. It was his wife's encouragement that kept him going.

Some months later, he got a call from his wife at work. A small publishing house had accepted the book, and they were offered him $2,500.

The book's first print couldn't sell well, so they sold it to a paperback publisher. That's when things changed completely. Within the first year, a million copies were sold. That rescued "trash" began a career, and it paved the way for him to write more than 60 books that have all hit the bestsellers list.

Failure could be a useful tool for success if you learn not to give up.[5,6]

Stephen King threw his fortune into the bin. It took his wife to rescue their fortune. As a researcher, who is your advisor, or whom do you receive encouragement from? Write down five people who are your advisors in your project.

_____

_____

_____

_____

If you meet rejections in the conduct of your project, will you give up? Why?

_____

_____

_____

CHAPTER 11

Be Determined to Finish Your Research Project

It will take great determination to complete your research project, especially when encountering many problems or failures. It has to do with your ability not to give up on your project. Usually, when you want to publish your paper, you might face many rejections from journals – sometimes up to five or more. You need to persist and seek expert advice to finish your project.

Determination is a positive mental character of not giving up on your goals despite difficulties. After you decide to conduct research, you may run into roadblocks and obstacles. If you master this skill, you will be determined to complete your project. You will focus your efforts and resources on sticking with it until the project is completed.[1]

If you are less determined, you will give up when things get hard. Determination is to succeed as oxygen is to life. It is a prerequisite for achieving great results. Every researcher that has great accomplishments did it with determination. The good news is that you can learn the skill of determination no matter how many times you have given up in the past.[2]

How will you rate yourself (1-10) on the ITA in terms of the following?

ITA indicators	Fair	Good	Very good	Excellent	Outstanding
Willing to commit					
Willing to work hard					
Willing to discipline yourself					
Ability to handle disappointment					
Willing to sacrifice					
Ability to handle failure					
Ability to persist/determination					

Scoring:
Fair-1; good - 2; very good - 3; excellent - 4; outstanding-5

The total score is 35 points

What's your score? _____

What do you need to do to improve your ITA score?

_____

_____

_____

_____

_____

_____

_____

SECTION III

The Ultimate Research Writing Formula

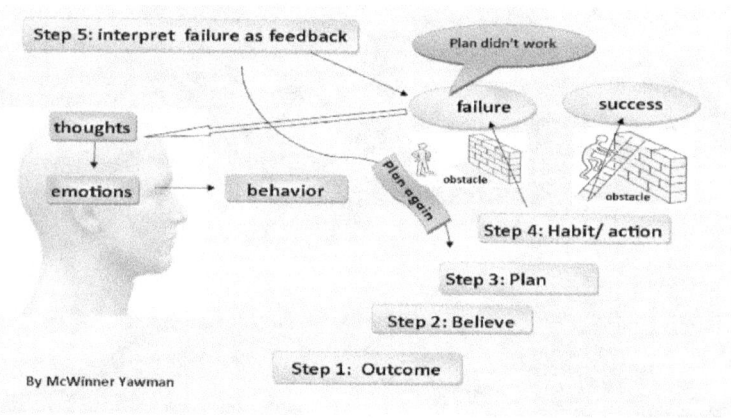

CHAPTER 12

Know Your Outcome

What problem do you want to solve with your research, and in what area or field specifically? What is it exactly that you want to find out or investigate?

The first step to achieving your research goal is to KNOW the problem you intend to solve through your research or the exact thing you want to investigate. It should be crystal clear to you. You should be very convinced within yourself why you have chosen to research that problem.

This is where your research problem and questions come in. A research problem is a statement about an area of concern, a condition to be improved, a difficulty to be eliminated, or a troubling question that exists in scholarly literature, in theory, or in practice that points to the need for meaningful understanding and deliberate investigation.

In some social science disciplines, the research problem is typically posed in the form of a question. A research problem does not state how to do something and offers up a vague or broad proposition. It should be specific and direct to the point. Whatever it is that you want to arrive with your study is your outcome. This outcome should be crystal clear to you.[1]

What is the outcome of your thesis?

_____

_____

_____

_____

_____

_____

_____

_____

_____

_____

CHAPTER 13

Believe You Can Complete Your Research Project

"Whether you think you can, or you think you cannot, either way, you are right" - Henry Ford. Believing you can finish your project within the stipulated time is very important.

The question is, "why must you finish your project outstandingly?" Your answer to this question must be compelling enough to drive you to take more action. What reward will you get after completion? On the other hand, what are the consequences of not completing? You MUST believe you will write an outstanding thesis at all costs.

The majority of potential researchers underestimate their abilities. Self-doubt could destroy the confidence you have in your ability. As a researcher, count yourself a failure only after completely giving up on all attempts to do research.

It should be otherwise; you should think positively about your ability. Thinking positive and empowering thoughts is one thing, but talking to yourself like a great innovator or inventor reconditions your thought process in an instant. When you form the habit of talking to yourself like a champion, you negate all discouraging thoughts and negative feelings.

Self-efficacy theory was developed within the framework of social cognitive theory.[1] Bandura poses self-confidence as a common cognitive mechanism for mediating motivation, thought patterns, emotional reactions, and behavior. The theory was originally proposed to account for the different results achieved by the diverse methods used in clinical psychology for treating anxiety.

Self-confidence is considered one of the most influential motivators and regulators of behavior in people's everyday lives. A growing body of evidence suggests that one's perception of ability or self-confidence is the central mediating construct of achievement strivings.[2]

How well do you believe in your ability to write a great research?

_____

_____

_____

_____

_____

On a scale of 1 to 10, how much will you rate yourself on your self-belief?

_____

_____

What needs to happen for you to believe you have what it takes to write a great research project?

_____

_____

_____

_____

_____

_____

_____

_____

CHAPTER 14

Make a Plan for Your Research Project

Whether your research is for a thesis or dissertation, it needs careful planning and organization. You will not be successful if you simply start work and then see where it leads.

An important factor that makes it vital to plan is the time frame and the financial component. It would be best if you start by thinking through the stages of your project.

You need an Action Plan which, when you look at it, you can say with certainty, "I'm going to achieve my outcome." It is a step-by-step plan you'll follow to conduct your research project.

With the Action Plan, you will know exactly what you need to do to achieve your goal. For example, if you are to finish your research project in 4 months, you will have to budget your time according to the key activities you need to undertake.

As a researcher making an action plan will help you navigate the whole process of your project with precision. The process of planning begins by taking a holistic view of the entire project. Review how much

72

time you have, your research goals, references, data sources, and the expertise at your disposal.

Cost Component

Task	Unit cost	Quantity	Total
Printing			
Proofreading/editing			
Data gathering			
Statistical analysis			
Etc.			

Tasking Component

Task	Assigned to	Resource person	Literature sources
Introduction			
Literature review			
Data gathering			
Data analysis			
Etc.			

Do you have an action plan for your thesis project?

_____

_____

_____

Example of a Research Action Plan

Task	Specific Action steps	Completion date	Task Assigned to	Potential barriers	Progress remarks
Title defense	How will the task be done?	By when?	Whom is the task assigned to	What could hinder success?	How far was the task completed?
Proposal defense					
Data collection					
Analyze data					
First draft					
Discuss draft with adviser					
Final defense					
Etc.					

CHAPTER 15

Take Massive Action on Your Research Project

Habits control action. If you don't take action, nothing will happen; this is where habits come in. Negative habits will prevent you from taking action. Once you make a plan, commit to following through. While taking action on your project, you will face problems or obstacles. Your ability to overcome them will bring you to SUCCESS OR FAILURE (FEEDBACK).

Celebrate if you write an outstanding thesis. On the other hand, if you receive feedback, especially at the defense of your thesis, there could be something you need to improve with your plan and method. Evaluate your method and retake more action to complete your thesis project.

There will be a need to evaluate your daily routines. How you use your time, especially during this period, is very important. You need to prioritize your commitments to have enough time to finish your thesis project.

Setting goals for your research project

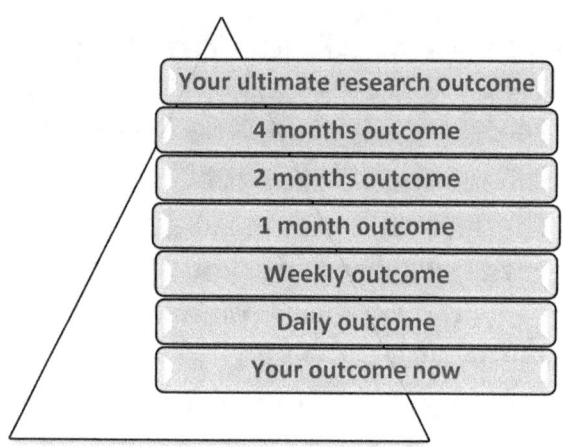

Monthly outcomes
Example:
This month I am committed to:
1. To make my questionnaires ready
2. Gather my data
3. Analyze the data
4. Etc….

Weekly Outcomes
Example

This week I am committed to:
1. Draft and revise my questionnaires
2. Meet three experts
3. Read five literature
4. Etc. ….

Daily Outcomes

Example

Today/tomorrow, I am committed to:

1. Meet my adviser by 10 am -11 am for some inputs on my questionnaires
2. Draft 35% of the questionnaire by 2:00-3:00 pm
3. Formulate the research problems
4. Etc.

How disciplined are you, when it comes to time management? Rate yourself from 1 to 10.

_____.

What needs to happen for you to take more action to complete your thesis project on time?

_____

_____

_____

_____

What are you going to do each day to complete your research project?

_____

_____

_____

_____

_____

_____

Remember, it is about what you do daily that will bring success to your project. You have to do something about your project every single day; finish every task assigned for the day without postponement. You will need to set daily goals and use a daily to-do list. Schedule every activity on your list every single day. This is important because if you don't schedule them, they will never be accomplished.

Some Time Management Tools and Techniques

Good time management is essential to the success of your project. By using an effective time planner and the master list, you can achieve any research goal you set. Using these standard time management tools and techniques will surely boost your productivity beyond measure:

1. Set daily or weekly goals

2. Use a time planner and create a to-do list

3. Always work from a list

4. Set priority on your list

5. Delegate every item you are not an expert at

6. Schedule every item on your list

7. Incorporate online time management tools and systems

8. Stay committed to your daily task and complete them

You may want to try a daily planner like the one below:

Time	Mon	Tue	Wed	Thu	Fri	Sat	Sun
6:00							
7:00							
8:00							
9:00							
10:00							
11:00							
12:00							
13:00							
14:00							
15:00							

CHAPTER 16

Celebrate Your Success or Interpret Feedback

At this stage, if you failed your thesis defense, you are thinking about what went wrong. You might be making mental pictures of what went wrong. As you think about it, you interpret it or attach meaning to it. Whatever your interpretation is, it creates your emotion. This is where most people quit and don't continue with their thesis.

The interpretation (the meaning you create) will create fear in you or give you the courage to try again. Your emotions will then create your behavior toward your thesis project. Now your behavior will be to QUIT, DO the SAME THING AGAIN OR USE ANOTHER PLAN/METHODOLOGY

The key here is "you must control your emotions to control your behavior." *Turn your failure into feedback.* If you have positive behavior, you can learn something from your plan/method that didn't work. _Now you need to get a plan that works (proven plan) or adopt a proven methodology_.

Do you have the tendency to abandon your project when problems come up?

_____

_____

What do you need to do so as not to give up on your project?

_____

_____

_____

_____

_____

_____

_____

_____

_____

_____

I offer special training based on this book to schools, colleges, and universities.

You may want me to visit your institution to get your faculty on track to begin the research projects. Thank you.

SECTION IV:
Effective Time for Researchers

CHAPTER 17

Effective Time Management For Researchers

Time management is the process of organizing and planning how to divide your time between specific activities.

Good time management enables you to work smarter, not harder so that you get more done in lesser time, even when time is tight and pressures are high. Failing to manage your time damages your effectiveness and causes stress.

Myths about Time Management

1. Time management is nothing but common sense. I do well in school, so I must be managing my time effectively.
2. It takes all the fun out of life!
3. Time management? I work better under pressure.
4. No matter what I do, I won't have enough time!

The Truth About Time Management

1. It increases productivity.

2. It reduces stress.
3. It improves self-esteem.
4. It helps achieve balance in life.
5. It increases self-confidence.
6. It helps you reach your goals.

Setting Priorities

	Urgent	Not Urgent
Important	**Quadrant I** • Crisis • Pressing problems • Deadline driven projects	**Quadrant II** • Relationship building • Finding new opportunities • Long-term planning • Preventive activities • Personal growth • Recreation
Not Important	**Quadrant III** • Interruptions • Emails, calls, meetings • Popular activities • Proximate, pressing matters	**Quadrant IV** • Trivia, busy work • Time wasters • Some calls and emails • Pleasant activities

Source: Steve Covey

Source: Steve Covey

Steps to Managing Your Time

1. Set goals
2. Set reasonable expectations (and remember that no one's perfect)
3. Make a schedule
4. Revisit and revise your plan

Revisit Your Values

Knowing what is most valuable to you gives direction to your life. Your energy should be oriented first toward things that reflect your most important values. Examine your values to help you make time management decisions.

Where to start? What is Important?

Make your goals specific and concrete, not vague. Set both your long-term and short-term research goals.

Set a deadline for your goals. Integrate your goals: school, personal, and career. Realize that goals change, but know which goals to stick to!

Set priorities

What's important and what's not important? In what order should things be done? Once you know your priorities, you need to plan out a schedule for the semester if you are in a school setting or for the month, week, and day

Acknowledge the realities of college schedules. Planning may seem hard at first, but the more you do it, the easier and more natural it gets.

Make a Schedule

Set up your semestral calendar. Allot time for all important obligations.

Organizing Your Time

Set realistic goals; there are only 24 hours in a day. Commit 2-3 hours per week to do some kind of research. Schedule it on your calendar.

Use a daily to-do list, weekly and monthly planner, whichever is applicable.

for Today...

DATE:_____

M T W T F S S

TODAY I AM GRATEFUL FOR:

TOP 3 GOALS:
1 _____ ☐
2 _____ ☐
3 _____ ☐

APPOINTMENTS
_____
_____
_____
_____
_____

DAILY TASKS/CLEANING
☐ _____
☐ _____
☐ _____
☐ _____
☐ _____

TO DO LIST:
☐ _____
☐ _____
☐ _____
☐ _____
☐ _____
☐ _____
☐ _____
☐ _____
☐ _____

FAVORITE VERSE/QUOTE,
TAKE NOTES, DRAW, JOURNAL, ETC:

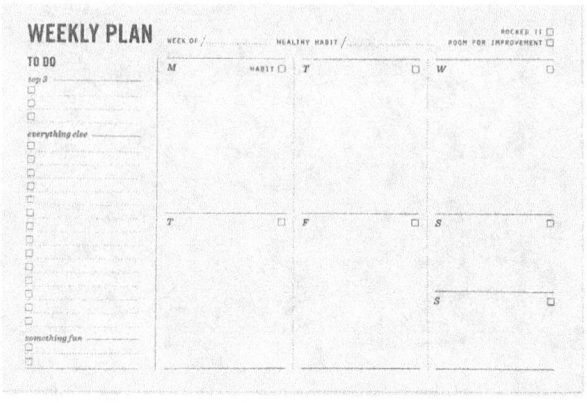

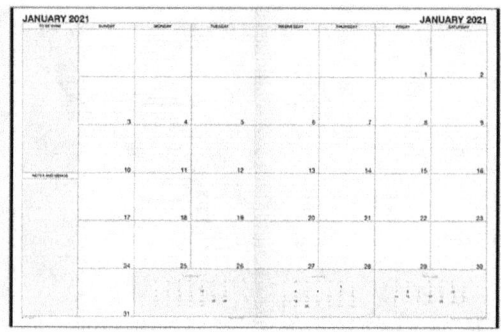

Evaluate your day

Guide questions

1. How are you using your time? Which tasks were you able to do?
2. What didn't get done?
3. Was your energy level appropriate? How about your stress level?
4. What changes need to be made to your weekly schedule?

5. What are persistent time wasters?
6. Was procrastination an issue?

How to Overcome Procrastination

1. Win the mental battle by committing to being on time.
2. Set and keep deadlines.
3. Organize, schedule & plan.
4. Divide a big job into smaller ones.
5. Please find a way to make a game of your work or make it fun.
6. Reward yourself when you're done.
7. Tell your friends and roommates to remind you of priorities and deadlines.
8. Learn to say "no" to time wasters.

How to Tackle Time Wasters

1. Learn to recognize when you're wasting time.
2. Decide what you need to do and can realistically do.
3. Learn how to say "NO" when you don't have time.
4. Return calls at your convenience. The phone is a major time killer.

5. Learn to say, "I can't talk right now. I'll get back to you."
6. Wasting time is often linked to a lack of self-discipline.
7. Ask yourself, "Do I need to do this or not?"

Learn to say "NO!"

Avoid the temptation to socialize when you've scheduled work. If friends ask you to join them last minute, decline outright, but ask if you could get together later in the week. Socializing is important when you don't have other things to worry about!

Work in a place you won't be tempted to chat, watch movies or YouTube or use social utilities like Facebook. Texts are a major distraction.

Tips For Managing Time Effectively

Time flies always. That makes time a variable that can be hard to control and monitor. And once time has slipped away, you never get it back.

Being conscious of time as a researcher will result in self-improvement and goal achievement. That's true in both your work and personal life.

1. Have a Time Check

Know exactly how you spend your time. In an office setting, you should know the tasks that are stealing your time so you can do something about it. For example, you may be spending an hour on email instead of completing important projects.

Knowing exactly where your time goes can help you decide about delegating tasks or putting measures in place to ensure effective use of your time.

Setting a time limit for a task can be fun; it can be like a game. To be productive in your research project, measure the time you spend every time you work on your research.

You can apply this principle to any task. Set a definite time limit, such as an hour or two. Then try to finish the task within the allotted time and feel the excitement as you do it.

3. Use Software Tools for Time Management

Technology is more sophisticated at managing time. Various apps help track your time so that you can monitor the progress of your research.

For many apps, the advanced functions of the paid versions can also give you added control and a better user experience. Listed below are some of the applications:

1. Time management apps
2. Todoist
3. Calendar
4. nTask
5. Be Focused Timer
6. Focus Booster
7. Kiwake App
8. Loop - Habit Tracker
9. Focus@Will
10. Freedom
11. Noisli
12. OmniFocus

13. Forest App
14. Asana
15. Toggl
16. Remember The Milk
17. Trello

4. Have a To-Do List

Having a list is always a time saver. If you have a list, you'll never have to wonder what's on the daily schedule or what to do next.

Indeed, a list keeps you focused and motivated, focused on a feeling of sweet satisfaction every time you tick off a task from your list.

Lists let you see and monitor your progress. Even if distractions surround you, your list will keep you on the right track.

5. Plan Ahead

Planning ahead is a critical part of time management. Ideally, you should plan ahead for the week or at least the day before.

You will stay organized and focused when you know exactly what needs to get done for the day or week.

You can break tasks across days to see how much time is needed to complete a project. Spending a few minutes planning ahead can transform how you work.

6. Start with Your Most Important Tasks

Do your most important tasks in the morning. You have the most energy in the morning so that you will tackle the tasks efficiently and competently.

Plus, the feeling of accomplishment at getting the most important stuff done first will make the rest of the day that much better.

7. Delegate and Outsource

You can't do everything by yourself, so cut yourself some slack and delegate. In doing research, always focus on the tasks you do best and delegate the rest. You don't have to be an expert at everything

8. Focus on One Task at a Time

If you have chosen to do a task, see it through to the end – finish it. Avoid doing half work, which means abandoning your current task and doing something else entirely.

One example of half-work is writing a report, then suddenly checking your email for no reason and writing replies. That's bad time management and bad for your concentration; you will lose your momentum. Focus on the task at hand, and avoid these pitfalls.

9. Make Some Changes in Your Schedule

If you feel more energized at certain times of the day, change your schedule to embrace that. Make the most of your time.

Some people are more energized in the morning, while some are night owls. When you choose the best schedule, you'll enjoy the benefits of being able to do more.

NOTES

Chapter 1

1. Encarta dictionary
2. James Allen

Chapter 2

1. http://www.businessdictionary.com/definition/attitude.html
2. https://www.forbes.com/sites/margiewarrell/2015/03/31/trainthebrave-2/#37286c304c31
3. https://www.lifehack.org/articles/productivity/6-effective-ways-to-become-persistent.html

Chapter 3

1. https://www.entrepreneur.com/article/225321
2. https://jamesclear.com/focus#What%20is%20Focus?
3. https://facilethings.com/blog/en/focus

Chapter 4

http://paidtoexist.com/go-all-out/

Chapter 5

https://medium.com/the-mission/hard-work-is-the-single-greatest-competitive-advantage-8e65a1e674f4

Chapter 7

1. https://www.positivelypresent.com/2015/02/how-to-handle-disappointment.html

2. https://www.huffpost.com/entry/overcome-disappointment_n_7625870

Chapter 8

1. https://www.goalcast.com/2018/05/24/4-sacrifices-successful-people-make/
2. https://www.lifehack.org/articles/productivity/8-things-successful-people-sacrifice-for-their-success.html

Chapter 9

1. https://www.theguardian.com/culture/2016/may/24/interview-james-dyson-vacuum-cleaner
2. https://www.developgoodhabits.com/successful-people-failed/
3. https://www.biography.com/people/thomas-edison-9284349
4. https://www.history.com/topics/inventions/thomas-edison
5. https://www.developgoodhabits.com/successful-people-failed/
6. https://www.riskology.co/one-success/

Chapter 10

1. https://www.school-for-champions.com/character/determination.htm#.XLj8hIlKjIU
2. https://motivationgrid.com/things-determined-people-dont-do/

Chapter 11

1. https://library.sacredheart.edu/c.php?g=29803&p=185918

Chapter 12

1. Bandura, A. (1999). A social cognitive theory of personality. In L. Pervin & O. John (Ed.), Handbook of personality (2nd ed., pp. 154-196). New York: Guilford Publications. (Reprinted in D. Cervone & Y. Shoda [Eds.], The coherence of personality. New York: Guilford Press.)
2. Bandura, A., & Cervone, D. (1986). Differential engagement of self-reactive influences in cognitive motivation. Organizational Behavior and Human Decision Processes, 38, 92-113;

3. Ericsson, K. A., Krampe, R. Th., & Tesch-Roemer, C. (1993). The role of deliberate practice in the acquisition of expert performance. Psychological Review, 100, 363-406.
4. Harter, S. (1978). Effectance motivation reconsidered: Toward a developmental model. Human Development, 21, 34-64. doi:10.1159/000271574;
5. Kuhl, P. K., Williams, K. A., Lacerda, F., Stevens, K. N., & Lindblom, B. (1992). Linguistic experience alters phonetic perception in infants by 6 months of age. *Science, 255*(5044), 606-608.
6. Nicholls, J. G. (1984). Achievement Motivation: Conceptions of Ability, Subjective Experience, Task Choice, and Performance. Psychological Review, 91, 328-346. https://doi.org/10.1037/0033-295X.91.3.328.

BIBLIOGRAPHY

1. http://www.businessdictionary.com/definition/attitude.html
2. https://www.forbes.com/sites/margiewarrell/2015/03/31/trainthebrave-2/#37286c304c31
3. https://www.lifehack.org/articles/productivity/6-effective-ways-to-become-persistent.html
4. https://www.entrepreneur.com/article/225321
5. https://jamesclear.com/focus#What%20is%20Focus?
6. https://facilethings.com/blog/en/focus
7. http://paidtoexist.com/go-all-out/
8. https://medium.com/the-mission/hard-work-is-the-single-greatest-competitive-advantage-8e65a1e674f4
9. https://www.positivelypresent.com/2015/02/how-to-handle-disappointment.html
10. https://www.huffpost.com/entry/overcome-disappointment_n_7625870
11. https://www.goalcast.com/2018/05/24/4-sacrifices-successful-people-make/
12. https://www.lifehack.org/articles/productivity/8-things-successful-people-sacrifice-for-their-success.html
13. https://www.theguardian.com/culture/2016/may/24/interview-james-dyson-vacuum-cleaner
14. https://www.developgoodhabits.com/successful-people-failed/
15. https://www.biography.com/people/thomas-edison-9284349
16. https://www.history.com/topics/inventions/thomas-edison
17. https://www.developgoodhabits.com/successful-people-failed/
18. https://www.riskology.co/one-success/

19. https://www.school-for-champions.com/character/determination.htm#.XLj8hIl KjIU
20. https://motivationgrid.com/things-determined-people-dont-do/
21. https://library.sacredheart.edu/c.php?g=29803&p=18 5918
22. Bandura, A. (1999). A social cognitive theory of personality. In L. Pervin & O. John (Ed.), Handbook of personality (2nd ed., pp. 154-196). New York: Guilford Publications. (Reprinted in D. Cervone & Y. Shoda [Eds.], The coherence of personality. New York: Guilford Press.)
23. Bandura, A., & Cervone, D. (1986). Differential engagement of self-reactive influences in cognitive motivation.
24. Organizational Behavior and Human Decision Processes, 38, 92-113;
25. Ericsson, K. A., Krampe, R. Th., & Tesch-Roemer, C. (1993). The role of deliberate practice in the acquisition of expert performance. Psychological Review, 100, 363-406.
26. Harter, S. (1978). Effectance motivation reconsidered: Toward a developmental model. Human Development, 21, 34-64. doi:10.1159/000271574;
27. Kuhl, P. K., Williams, K. A., Lacerda, F., Stevens, K. N., & Lindblom, B. (1992). Linguistic experience alters phonetic perception in infants by 6 months of age. Science, 255(5044), 606-608.
28. Nicholls, J. G. (1984). Achievement Motivation: Conceptions of Ability, Subjective Experience, Task Choice, and Performance. Psychological Review, 91, 328-346. https://doi.org/10.1037/0033-295X.91.3.328

29. https://www.mindtools.com/pages/article/newHTE_00
.htm

www.ingramcontent.com/pod-product-compliance
Lightning Source LLC
Chambersburg PA
CBHW060414290526
45791CB00002B/749